brash ice

Critical Praise for the books of Djelloul Marbrook

Artemisia's Wolf

...successfully blends humor and satire (and perhaps even a touch of magic realism) into its short length ...an engrossing story, but what might strike the reader most throughout the book is its infusion of breathtaking poetry...a stunning rebuke to notoriously misogynist subcultures like the New York art scene, showing us just how hard it is for a young woman to be judged on her creative talent alone.

—Tommy Zurhellen, *Hudson River Valley Review*

Saraceno

...Djelloul Marbrook writes dialogue that not only entertains with an intoxicating clickety-clack, but also packs a truth about low-life mob culture The Sopranos only hints at. You can practically smell the anisette and filling-station coffee.

—Dan Baum, author of *Gun Guys* (2013) and *Nine Lives: Mystery, Magic, Death and Life in New Orleans* (2009) and others

...a good ear for crackling dialogue ... I love Marbrook's crude, raw music of the streets. The notes are authentic and on target ...

—Sam Coale, *The Providence (RI) Journal*

...an entirely new variety of gangster tale ... a Mafia story sculpted with the most refined of sensibilities from the clay of high art and philosophy ... the kind of writer I take real pleasure in discovering ...a mature artist whose rich body of work is finally coming to light."

—Brent Robison, editor, *Prima Materia*

Far from Algiers

...as succinct as most stanzas by Dickinson... an unusually mature, confidently composed first poetry collection.

—Suzanna Roxman, *Prairie Schooner*

...brings together the energy of a young poet with the wisdom of long experience.

—Edward Hirsch, Guggenheim Foundation

Brushstrokes and Glances

Whether it is commentary on state power, corporate greed, or the intensely personal death of a loved one, Djelloul Marbrook is clear-sighted, eloquent, and precise. As the title of the collection suggests, he uses the lightest touch, a collection of fragments, brushstrokes and glances, to fashion poems that resonate with truth and honesty.

—Phil Constable, *New York Journal of Books*

brash ice

poems by

Djelloul Marbrook

LEAKY BOOT PRESS

Brash Ice
by Djelloul Marbrook

Acknowledgments

"woodstock" first appeared in *Fledgling Rag* No. 10
"after image" first appeared in *Pirene's Fountain*, April 2013

First published in 2014 by
Leaky Boot Press
http://www.leakyboot.com

ISBN: 978-1-909849-15-0

for David L. O'Melia
and George B. Donus

The vision is not so much destroyed, exactly,
as it is, by the time you have finished, forgotten.
It has been replaced by this changeling.

—Annie Dillard

contents

proem

i'd be not there

i'd make athena blink

i'd witness the sidelong world

i'd lay my own ashes

i'd study brash ice

Brash ice is broken ice that appears
scarred after freezing again.

proem

handling plutonium

so this business of being you
is about handling plutonium
and is much more dangerous
than your parents said.
you stumbled across yourself so often
you became your own nightmare
and then one day the sun rose
on a world where winners and losers
cast no shadows. you saw no choice
but to turn your back on the game,
to remake the world with your painterly eye,
to be a forensic sculptor, to let
intellect's luminol reveal
what fears can't bleach,
to stare at the consequences
even as they throw dirt on your face.

if i had a painterly eye

here's what i would do to celebrate,
i'd show me atoms of something else
in the manner of seurat or tanguy,
a congress of memories,
a sufferance like frankenstein's beast
becoming more than its parts
hankering to fulfill their longings,
i'd witness the sidelong world,
i'd lay my own ashes,
i'd make athena blink.
i'd study brash ice.
failing that i'd call failure life
& unmask myself as a firefly
nobody caught in a jar.

escapade

how i change you with a look
signals our painterly lives,
colors we make of memories,
canvas bared to reticence,
dilutions spelling scent,
solutions ecstatic in themselves.
i take the task seriously,
i'm able to correct my work
and i know its pentimento
will be explored. snapshots
never interested me, nor beauty
agreed upon by voyeurs.
i like inspired mistake,
a peripheral glance that jars
our nerve ends loose,
diseases that best define
our escapades at being well.

i'd be not there

rehearsals begin

you rubbed your face before turning out the light;
in the morning you found you'd rubbed it off.
you stared at your hands but they were no help,
your old face was gone and in its place
was the little boy you once had been.
the long night was over, the day begun,
and with it rehearsals of not being there.

softly

yield me fiercely to this undertaking,
this flowering of pain, this milling
of memory and bone. laugh
when my golden dust reconstitutes itself
and hurls the grindstone hurtling
through majesties of trees in a kind of youth
that mocks ever having to grow old
until the next time and perhaps the one time
when i will remember everything softly.

where are you now?

will you love me forever & ever,
cross your heart and hope to die?
he took the hope-to-die part seriously
& to do that he had to cross his heart
again & again not knowing once you do
it becomes your unbecoming.
you were capable of love,
having no idea what it was
or what was to come—
the future was a bother,
the past a sore. you gladly fell
into the well of her eyes
and never climbed out,
& when she left you found
she had taken you with her.

dear friend

you don't leave much for the undertaker

so fully you've inhabited there
i've never minded your not being here
you being a favorite hallucination
but i wonder how you speak of us

the lives you've brushed off your sleeve
have not gone unnoticed in their journey
to the floor but if i'd told you i'd seen them
it would have dissolved our friendship
as surely as if i'd stopped drinking
and when i stopped you were already leery
of my having seen too much and i was pissed
at having to camouflage my ardent voyeurism

whose fault is it that what drew us
scared us unready to be freaks
as we were and how could you not smell
of the bed sheets of other planets
and how could you hide the milky ways
that swarmed your eyes

do you approve
of my remarks now that they matter so little
or do you propose to leave under cover
as you have lived here gingerly and alert
to witch-hunters and the un-american activities committee
partying in every other head?

you were unable to forget where you'd been
i was unable to renounce vestigial gifts
how could we not be friends and how
could we not threaten good ole boys
and other swaggering pretenders
women set on being offended dogs
hell-bent on chumminess and kids
persuaded of their charm

how
could we survive the poor theater
that fears anton chekov and depends
on lighting and cheap violence for effect

now you are past caring and stare
out upon the sound as if a viking pyre
awaits you i wish only this for you
that you never again have to explain yourself
to beguiling inquisitors like me

to ease life's rush

it's the disappearances that kill us.
viruses, bacteria and bullets
are vaudeville, it's the disappearances
that grind our features off
to ease life's rush over us.
to bear such loss we vanish
so to not embarrass ourselves.

rain

somebody let up
warm rain fell
i fell asleep
when i awoke
someone had died
one less mind
to stir embers
to send sparks
up dry trees

batiks of our fondest ties

mind gone
   mine always going somewhere
beyond molestation and mistrusted beauty
beyond somewhere that never seemed
far enough
   mind gone that never fully came
with me to the squall i angled into
but remained without as i was to live
where belonging is too strange to fathom
   the problem with wanting us dead
is that we can never be dead enough
   beat this game by not being there
then again that is just what they suspect
and so the problem of stamping us out
(by the mere flutter of a wing or post
of an ill-making thought) is addictive
   this is the world of last hours live them
as if you had never seen anything before
   will i be welcome among the dead
will i intrude speak the language
look acceptable dodge the checkpoints
fake my papers and double down
on getting by and slipping past?

no and no because
we come off on each other
stains of our encounters
wranglings of our tied dyes
batiks of our fondest ties

what really pisses her off

he had taken up very little space
so it was easy to dispose of him
but not his amazing career
as an afterimage tampering
with synapses expected to fire
in predictable ways & now
emblazoning his bothering self
on the news of the moment in a room
that seems crowded & charred.

try as they do afterimages cannot report
the mischief & longing they incite
to their original owners, and would
those owners want to know it if they could?
the truth would tie one shoe to the other
& we'd trip on our own leavings,
we'd topple into space and burn up
leaving our apartments in the morning.

she doesn't know what she wants to know
except that once it was and wasn't him
& now he's operating in the room
and in her head like a rogue gene
& it would shame her to tell anyone
that what really pisses her off
is that he never asked for permission.

burning paper ships

these paper ships i light
hold eventualities.
i have no use for them.
insurance is too high,
tariffs too steep.
but a man without them,
where has he to go
except to be an ashen sheet
on a pond transected
by a heron's leaving?

just as if i had never heard

for a moment my fingers understood
all that i had never understood
and each key struck a note
as exciting as looking up
and seeing the lord god bird soar
for the first time and being sure
i knew how to play the piano
in spite of all i don't know
when i pretend to be awake—
a concert piano in an empty hall
where all the recognitions perch
that were once taught out of me

so much that i know how to do
& am no longer persuaded not to do
& so much pretending
i no longer have to do
because i have seen the lord god bird
and made unheard of music
just as if i had never heard
anyone pronounce my name

down the drain

and if i do look in a mirror and see nothing
might i ascend and not grow fangs,
drink the lord's blood and not yours
and rest awhile on thermals of your breath?
what if i could not hold myself together
long enough to admire my suffering
and flushed with my maunderings
down the drain instead of flitting
in wonderings of not being there?

i'd make athena blink

momentary delights

if life to life remembering enemies' scent
we look for that one priestess to touch
that one nerve that exposes the holidays
as commercial mileposts and explodes
the illusion of a quickening race, how
shall we not abandon kind to please her
and with what sort of mind judge success?
will her lopsided grin and lefthandedness
or her riveting gaze at the back of our heads
dispel time's trudging myth and undress
our tired bones of their history and histories
of their religious lies? and how will scent
help us to recognize that one priestess
in the milky way of pleasure and dismay?

something you enjoyed before

if i give this or that of me to you
will it regenerate
and how much of what i want to do
will you take to bed with you?

is it something only sensed you want
or something you enjoyed before,
and have you thought i might be dying
of withholding it from you?

is it that we know this much
that causes us to look and look away
because we can't remember
what we're supposed to do?

if we're dying of each other,
dying of what we finally see,
dying of our secret nakedness,
will it comfort us to sing?

galadriel's forest

black flames dance between exclamation marks,
blindnesses asking for the baptist's head.
a hand muffles my whisper,
i'm forced to the ground.

white birch trapped in diamonds and pearls,
my job applications are moldy leaves.
dead women shake me down,
foghorns call them home.

once i knew the differences between snow crystals,
i counted them for fun, but now the more
similarities deceive me the less
the forest seems like home.

this marvelous disease

your face pulls the tides of sirius
but is curious enough to visit us;
and as for yours, history staggers
under its casual gaze.
what am i to do, having spotted you,
what authorities do i report you to?
who cares who believes me? no pharmacy
has a pill for this dangerous disease,
since i have chosen it for my death
and live so well dying of it.

that one person

i have never been that one person without whom
ta-da ta-da ta-da, but i have known a few
who fill the room and think attention's due.

they are all i refuse to celebrate. i will not be a moth
no matter how cold the dark. i am content
that a star should be a mothhole in eternity.

demons, take your seats

it was urgent that i speak,
demons, take your seats,
so that the inevitable
might be postponed
until this distant day
when shutting up would seem
a bargain and i would wink
at your patient horrors
knowing i am one of you.

two dark wishes

the only people i wish in hell
    are those who always know what to say
now, exhibitionists, i'd like to torture them
    my animosities
tease orchids to bloom
    the only people i distrust
have no scent in tight circumstance
    blank mirrors don't trouble me
even angels can't count the cost of invisibility
    tell me more i don't know,
i'll tell you this, plants lean towards me
    in fear i have somewhere to go
as for grudges, plant in clusters
    beneath the frost, mulch with dismay
note everyone's shadow
    as do the bass the heron's, and think
if you think of me at all
    i did not steal the light from your face

the skipping stone

everything that was supposed to happen,
savage expectancy storming the eye
like gnats on an august evening,
somehow happened behind your back
to the shadows in your window.
why are you standing outside
as if you don't remember the house,
or have i interrupted a voyeur
who happens to look like you?
these haunts where dimensions elide,
cops and truckers and snipers know them—
the tail of the snake vanishing in the rocks,
comets drawing great beasts' blood,
and you wanting the harm behind the tree.
you were born inside out and my job
is to hurt you into life so that you may say
something happened to someone
even if you can't remember where
or to whom it may have happened.
the sad exudations of our many selves
tatter in the dusk and we go home
as if we knew where home is
as improvisations of bones.
nothing is going to happen, because you happened
on the stone of uncaring and sent it skipping
six times across the reflecting pool
the ways boys do to disturb complacencies
that threaten to become all there is.

the glory of snakes

i asked you if you liked wildflowers
& you said yes & then the devil got into me
& and i asked you if you liked snakes
& then we could not hold the planets in their circuits
for our fear of each other—you like serpents,
i pray rope not to come alive
& we love wildflowers not enough
to get by what winds in them.
you could have waffled but thought it important not to,
i could have lied, and there is the glory of snakes,
how hard it is to lie about them.

defiance

to celebrate the fragility of life
i call the living by the names of the dead,
i summon the living to a satanic mass
and hold the planets in my hand
until my wife throws me out of bed.
to celebrate the fragility of life
i drink too much of the absurd,
chew the logos like an olive
and like the pimento of the word.
to call the living by the names of the dead
is less a memory lapse than defiance
of everything our parents ever said.

passenger birds like me

it's not such a big deal
but if you're gonna go soft on me
i'm gonna open up your scars
& piss in them for old time's sake
like i used to do before you knew
everything in new york is serious.

but if you need to whine & cling
do it north of tappan zee
where the tree-killers live
& shit in our water
because they think we're having fun.
are we having fun?

you don't even know
because you wanna make a big deal
outta every kindness
birds drop on your nose,
passenger pigeons like me
going anywhere you can't imagine
so intent are you on you.

a taxidermied old sot

oh hello darling & things
i'm calling to ask if that painting
you know the one i sold you
of the lion with a boy on a leash
has been sold for what
oh i see & for how much
no not to whom dear.
when? well, no wonder
yes the one with the lion.
i have a client who loves boys,
a smelly old sot
taxidermied to a fare-thee-well,
little boys with or without
lions, yes darling we must.
ciao, ciao, love & all that,
we'll have a little drinky poo
& i'll tell you where i put bill
after that awful incident
i must before i forget.

holding my hand as i die

i never trusted anyone i liked
or liked anyone i trusted,
and here he is, my trusted son,
holding my hand as i die—
how bitter for us both!
it's not a mean accomplishment
to acknowledge this at death,
but what good will it do
in the morning for him or for you?

beauty and unrest

dutch clover thrives on lies,
well, yours anyway,
but weeds, i notice, not so much.

soil needs oxygen;
i'm still gasping for mine;
i yield nothing pure or white.

everything that scuttles
across your headstone
rings in my ears.

i am a symphony
of what is happening to you
in your grave.

next year, irish moss,
not so brazen, may
secrete a bouquet of stars

and i will bear witness
as i always have
to the marriage of beauty and unrest.

do not ask

i will bring to you everyone you need,
i will bring you to everyone you need
if only you do not ask me who i am.
i will teach you to swim in the eye of desire
and not drown, i will teach you to reemerge
as the thousands you have been before
and then to bind sheaves of comets
to light the corridors of my mind.

i'd witness the sidelong world

the testament of body hairs and scents

bees understand the electrical fields of flowers
but we prefer to act like marbles
even when our body hairs and scents
perform 'le sacre du printemps' in paris
when our druthers threaten us.
each physical truth is punishable
by a religion or two, a marriage
of convenience between scared fools,
a war, a class action suit
against the one good idea nobody
wants to hear. civilization rests
on our ignorance of electrical fields
and if our colonies were to collapse
perhaps we'd find we're not as vital as bees.

frisking the periphery

being a ninety-degree camera,
all i miss is straight ahead.
i adjust for light and flash,
i zoom to sync my paranoia.
you look as if you're being shot,
but i'm frisking the periphery.
everything behind my subject
is in focus, but the foreground
breeds misunderstanding.

i'm not interested in set-up shots
but hardly ever miss a set-up.
i am so hot for ambiguity
i usually miss the obvious.
i understand the nature of surfaces;
they never get under my skin,
but what is underneath dements me.
i am the green wink of chagrin
simply because i have no trash bin.

a gear or two

children hate me except the ones who don't.
i didn't scavenge such knowledge cheaply
or catch the absurd feeling up truth
by keeping my eye on the prize
because i never knew what it was
and always focused on the periphery
insofar as that can be done
without losing a gear or two.

habitué

when you're glad to see someone you don't know
you can measure how much of you survived the night.
his hand is not shaking today, he goes straight
to the counter unaware of inspiring you
to grope through the gloom in the meager hope
of lighting on another face as a butterfly takes
sustenance while stirring a hurricane or saving
a polar bear from drowning because of a misstep.
because of him there is a misstep you won't make,
and if he would think you mad for telling him
that would say what is precarious is exquisite
and you must keep it to yourself until
permission arrives from a white crane in siberia
and wafts across your thigh like a wish.

when clerks look through me

how will i smell to the gods
and their lesser consultants?
what prism will they use
to pick my light apart?

how to be honest with them,
will it matter by then?
will sophia present me
saying i've been ardent enough?

will i have the good sense
to keep my mouth shut
and my right hand and my eyes
as still as a night heron?

if color, as goethe said,
is the suffering of light
will i be fey enough
to fare blithely here

another time if asked
and must i forget
each object is an artifact
of pain, each pound defeat?

i am near to the gods
when clerks look through me;
why should i quarrel
with such transparency?

woodstock

what did i foresee
when daisies were permitted here?
i saw that i would know him,
this old man regarding me.

courtney rodney swigging moonshine
and telling me about the stars,
the milkman calling me a little wop
and becoming a famous actor,
woozy killing a rattlesnake
and sucking venom from my leg—
me, crazy for his sister.

my mother painting naked women—
bare-assed disappointment
even then seemed trite.
botox grins remind me
of wagnerian cashiers
ripping off my food stamps.

exquisite magda
feeding swans and hating jews;
i foresaw not wanting her
and tasted hope.

the other side

nothing was where it is
in such a glamored town
and they were never there
to remember anything.

this is the other side
of that and a slight tilt
of the mirrors turns
them all to otherlings.

nowhere to turn,
turning dislocates them,
sleep hides their parents
and them from themselves.

hometowns lead away
or poison apothecaries
that cure them of their gifts,
lead away from bloodhounds

and leeches acquired
in their flight from this
nothing blessedly left
where the children found it.

that kind of beauty

i made a geometric,
i could not add a thing,
not according to that esthetic
that penetrates the object
but finds no other side.
my gaze is lost in what i make,
i don't want it back,
i don't ask for a report.
it warms my feet at night,
haunts me in a sob;
did it ever belong to me,
can i count it as a loss?
not a perfect geometric
but something more than harm
that drowns the light
in certain people's eyes,
the kind of beauty
that sops up the night.

here your trajectory

here your solid trajectory
is cut up into intervals
and a handsome stranger
questions you in a basement

here your name fails you
your history dissolves
in beads of sweat
on a polished desk

where neurons unravel
a handsome stranger appears
with instruments of undoing
as disquieting as love

twig

if i ask you not to spring to life
what evil favor did i ask myself
that endows a locust twig with dread?

i have no heart for answers, but the question
does not suggest a wasted life
or settle fimbulwinter in my toes.

after image

images enfold each other
until everyone is a rose
whose ancient scent reminds
others not to look too long
for fear one may look too deep.

ghosts are projections of the eye
that cannot sort themselves
from their many lives, depending
on the light of our minds
to make their way in the dark.

whoever sees how populous we are
knows how futile it is to love,
since to love is to love a syzygy of souls
that only occasionally align
to celebrate an illusion of one.

when new york is under water

you know that look
i am dying are you god
is there hope
in elevators
& grimy cafés—
proof you've lived for something—
something others see
through cataracts
something to inform the light
when new york is under water?

but for the last time as men

i became a germ chimera
in a shudder of origami
in a shop always vacant
the day after. then i became
a day after bereft
of my shape-memory
or any connection
to the recognitions
that once informed me

& as a germ chimera longed
to be that mere shudder
of the cut & folded
origami of days,
to be that vacancy
the day after some event
but not the event, no,
i never wanted to be that
or anything obligating me
to belong and, belonging,
to sing in the choir,

because i knew my song,
my hymn, if you will,
would animate the statues,
blow away memories,
call back the gods
& pipe the monsters
with whom we sleep
so that we finally own
our deadliest names
& see each other nakedly
not for the first time
but for the last time as men.

i'd lay my own ashes

let me not run away to die

a cure grows two feet from a poison
let me not run away to die
or despise the beauty of either one
let me become invisible
to the cutters and diggers
& explicators every one
let me not run away to die
but take the cure to life
whether i must rub it on
or drink it down let me not run
to die among delusions
but live secure in knowledge
if only half understood
i was given all i need

carrots still to pull

concord grapes and dew,
carrots still to pull,
daisy and dolly nuzzling
a boy at his homework
in a frozen barn—
that's the innocence
waking an old man up
with such fragrances,
such exuberances
he might have thought
he had another life to live
had it not been for the pain
of not remembering a day
when he felt safe in bed.

bastard child

a man who remembers every day
makes money out of shit and pulls
lightning down to cauterize
his roots. if he could lose but one
and i knew which one it would be
i would plant it in hellebore
and ask white owls to mind
the birth of his bastard child.

being dead

don't talk to me from other rooms
not only because i'm hard of hearing
but because i don't want to be reminded
of those who counted on being misunderstood.
they didn't say what they meant,
they didn't mean what they said,
they needed to be misunderstood
and were offended by whatever i said,
and now between my bad ear and their being dead
i aim to enjoy the intermission,
i aim to cut their tethers in these last days
of star beasts partying in my head.

wild arts

memories, places,
their cosmologies,
what will happen
to them when i go?
i don't like to pick flowers
or jerk moments
from their haunts,
but who will revel in them?

i should worry more
that ego wants to slide
wild arts under glass,
wants to be the glass
through which others see
exquisites that become
as my ashes will
particular tomorrows.

i think the wildest art
is that as revelers
we are witnesses
to everything we chose
to revel in and thus
are born engulfed
in vast nostalgia
for the dead.

bolt

this couple riveting me,
not the usual exhibitionists...
my imminent departure
ticketed upon my face
instills envy reminding them
of all they have to do
and still must face.

may i give them energy
wasted on flirting shades,
gifts left in washrooms
and things not said,
anything to reward
their brave bolt
from bland pursuits?

the good in us

what smells good in this house?
tell us its olfactory history,
the secrets in its scents tell us
what ekes into the wood and plaster
and to which death was preferable.
tell us what tastes good in that house
or why nothing ever did, tell us

what delectations feed the rats
or why the rot is beautiful.
what is sharp, acrid or poisonous
doesn't concern us; sacred knowledge
is what we're after, the odor of desire
after one hundred years in the grave,
that kind of thing, lost pleasures

the good in us might be able to return.
and if this should seem impossible
we could try harder to make bankers rich
or imagine a world without shadows,
a world impossible to haunt,
the perfect freedom of the incurious,
and then who would want to hunt us?

finally passing for human

what it has taken to keep the boy alive
could have been used to make a poem.
each of us is an epiphany and a stone
in a river bed, and rushing over us
a roaring calculus ferrets to the sea.

i wear this boy like a rented suit.
i watched them try to lynch him, i saw him raped,
and when he finally passed for human
he said he was sorry he couldn't take me with him,
flicked a tear from me with his thumb, and left.

one old lady smiling

I can't seem to say anything
    that interests anyone
meeting here for purposes unknown to me
    in this village made of if
lined with forbidden realms
    apparent to the dead

except for one old lady smiling
    at everything I say
and so I conclude I came
    to discover her story
and walk her home
    to the cemetery

how golems are made

i pack my parts for shipping
to the lawless tribal area
where mercenaries pluck
emeralds from dead bodies
and buy whores with my eyes.

on this island of compartments
i bury my treasures in bellies
and forget to whom they belong
in order to be someone's demon.
so it is with us profligates.

i think this is how golems are made
losing pieces of themselves until
it doesn't matter what they're supposed to be
now that people pass through them
and ideas are nuisances.

does the current rest?

not even a hard life
entitles me to ask
but i think i will reclaim
my ashes from the ocean,
i will borrow me again,
i will be happy for it,
it will remind me
that once i forgot myself
and called it death,
that life i lived in dread—
that was the current's rest.

watchful child

i crawl into bed knees first, like a child
or a soldier under a hail of tracers;
i don't trust the world to be there for my ass
nor do i sleep on my back where they can get me,
they being you and other ogres of the night,
nor can i sleep with my heart exposed;
my side sinister, my bastard side, is what is left,
and there my right eye searches the terrain
for any dreams that might go over to the enemy
before i wake. i will die a watchful child.

as if i had merely dreamed

she could have been shot six miles away
and come here to die like a fond wish.
he would have tracked blood drops
until he grew tired or lost the trail.
i dragged her corpse across the icy field,
slipping, falling, much as i dragged
the dead bodies of bright moments
to some less than appropriate place,
the family clean-up man, souvenir
of my mother's youthful indiscretion.
i felt more pity for this doe than for anyone
who ever came my way to die, honored
but wondering why, why
she had come to me to die,
to close a circle i can't even draw,
to recall me to mortuarial duties
as if i had merely dreamed
of love marriage ambition life.

as i have among humans here

there was my own next life
drawing lines between the stars
in anticipation of a final shape,
there in clouds' womb wondering
if any more would be learned
by being another kind of beast,
a chimera of lights, a daemon
gamboling among universes
as i have among humans here.

what i have to work with

i don't want to behave like this again,
this being any way i have ever behaved,
nor like anyone i have ever read about
no matter how much i might have admired him,
nor do i want to be a man or woman again
but rather an androgyne who has no habits.

i don't want to become like this again
after so much heartfelt unbecoming,
all this tedium and plot. i haven't even got
a scent to contribute to the flowering
whose warmth i feel through the tunnel ahead.
i should have lost my soul in books.

i tried but it proved a handy figment:
what's death but what i have to work with now?

i'd study brash ice

the machineries of ice

once i saw the submarine's aerial
i knew it would always be like that,
picking through ice floes alert
to signals in a foreign language.

i knew the water would tremble
before the emergence of trouble,
radio silence would be imposed
and the machine gun would jam.

i wanted to send blueberries,
admire their uniforms, hope
for the best in the dark,
but they remembered their orders

even if i'd forgotten mine—
we hadn't come to make friends
but to numb our childish minds
on the machineries of ice.

brash ice

as ice closes the river the cities of my mind
nod out and sleep and this beast
shakes them off one by one lumbering
north to an unbearable light promising
to cure his incurable colors

he will jump on top of the world
with icebreakers in his fists and glower
at the flirtations of the stars

i don't know what else to say
because if i can will the ice i will
and then there will be no need to say
anything or sing against the wind
that keeps me back from where i should
and keys my bones with loneliness

i've said too much and said it flatly
because i thought the song pretentious
that splinters the wardrobe of the years
and shoves me out the door a naked stranger

snow crystals

i dreamed of counting snow crystals, diatoms and stars,
but all i could count on is you,
light without its maddening colors, you
without the prism of my mind to parse
the eyes you've lit in the crunching dark,
dreamed nothing escaped my notice,
a childhood given back to me
by a penitent demon in the wood,
a sorrow pool in which you bathe
innocent of my parents' thoughts.

icy foreign womb

you can't fly if you eat
history becomes flypaper
and if you forget your dreams
you will bleed out by evening
of the thirtieth year of your life—
that's all the time you have
to recover what was stolen
while you gathered yourself
in that icy foreign womb

to lie down in the snow

dogs sniff out lousy lovers,
detain them at the airports
to save you from people like me,
people hard-wired to leave
you with your expectations
measuring a liter of chagrin.
but what is it in wolves
that gives us losers a pass?
they recognize sorrow's scent,
who's ready to lie down in the snow
and give them our permission
to eat our disappointments,
to honor us, to let us go.
how do i know about wolves?
loping over the steppes of my mind
i become the spook of their stare.

the ash tree's scrawl

a dead man said goodbye to that barn;
can this be told by its looks?
what can an ash tree's shadow
etched on the moon tempera of the roof
tell a passerby of that man's sorrow
at having to leave his scythe and rake?

everyone is a ghost of someone else,
everything is ghosted—dogs and children
know this, and soundlessly we understand
the languages of the carbon community
to which the word belong belongs,
in which belonging is a crime.

the redwing reading by swamp lights knows
the dead man comes to the barn to sleep
because the days are hard on his eyes.

to come home starving

to come home starving
as the faerie xylophones
of the ice forest lift
knowledge of where home is
is all i know of journey,
all i imagine of death.
after many banquets
to come home starving
would be impolite unless
i wasn't expecting to be fed.
do you recognize me,
am i mistaken, do you
mistake me for one
who ignored the music?

to come home starving,
sick of snow and glaciers
scouring the brain,
depositing bodies' moraine
in our front yards
is an affront. we intended
to love you in absentia
and here you are,

loud dogs' bones
when we prefer the fat.
what evil compass
returns you to us
with your strange reports?
did we deserve this honor—
templars looking like saracens?

my old age

my thoughts are frail mobsters
guarded by bracioles in suits.
sometimes they wear pajamas
under pinstriped jackets
and chat with cops in gibberish.

i am deadlier than i used to be
in wily, goo-goo ways, deadlier
than the child who worried
if the shabtis in the museum
would have enough to eat.

in back of over and beyond

death is a cold rain in aspen groves
undersides otherlings underthings
in back of over and beyond
or life itself and this is waiting
in an anteroom

CPSIA information can be obtained
at www.ICGtesting.com
Printed in the USA
FFOW03n1207161215
19388FF